Animals in the...

Zoo

Siân Smith

raintree

Raintree is an imprint of Capstone Global Library Limited, a company incorporated in England and Wales having its registered office at 7 Pilgrim Street, London, EC4V 6LB – Registered company number: 6695582

www.raintreepublishers.co.uk
myorders@raintreepublishers.co.uk

Text © Capstone Global Library Limited 2015
First published in hardback in 2014
Paperback edition first published in 2015
The moral rights of the proprietor have been asserted.

Edited by Siân Smith, John-Paul Wilkins and Helen Cox Cannons
Designed by Cynthia Akiyoshi
Picture research by Mica Brancic and Tracy Cummins
Production by Victoria Fitzgerald
Originated by Capstone Global Library
Printed and bound in China

ISBN 978 1 406 28050 0 (hardback)
18 17 16 15 14
10 9 8 7 6 5 4 3 2 1

ISBN 978 1 406 28055 5 (paperback)
19 18 17 16 15
10 9 8 7 6 5 4 3 2 1

British Library Cataloguing in Publication Data
A full catalogue record for this book is available from the British Library.

Acknowledgements
We would like to thank the following for permission to reproduce photographs: Shutterstock pp. 1 (© belizar), 2 (© MaZiKab), 3 left, 20 top middle (© Eric Isselee), 3 middle, 20 top right (© Talvi), 3 right, 20 top left (© Aaron Amat), 4 (© Andrey Burmakin), 5 (© Tomo), 6 (© Anan Kaewkhammul), 7 (© Lynn Whitt), 8 (© Galina Barskaya), 10 (© Fotokon), 11, 22b (© worldswildlifewonders), 12, 22a (© Anthony Cooper), 13 (© Nicola Colombo), 14 (© babetka), 15 (© lunatic67), 16 (© enciktat), 17, 21 (© Hung Chung Chih), 18 (© Seleznev Oleg), 19 (© tratong), 20 bottom left (© Vadim Petrakov), 20 bottom middle (© Villiers Steyn), 20 bottom right (©kanate).

Front cover photograph of a giraffe reproduced with kind permission of Shutterstock (© belizar).

Every effort has been made to contact copyright holders of material reproduced in this book. Any omissions will be rectified in subsequent printings if notice is given to the publisher.

Contents

Zoo animals

Look at the elephant.

Look at the monkey.

Look at the tiger.

Look at the lion.

penguin

Look at the penguin.

Look at the seal.

Look at the polar bear.

Look at the koala.

Look at the crocodile.

hippo

Look at the hippo.

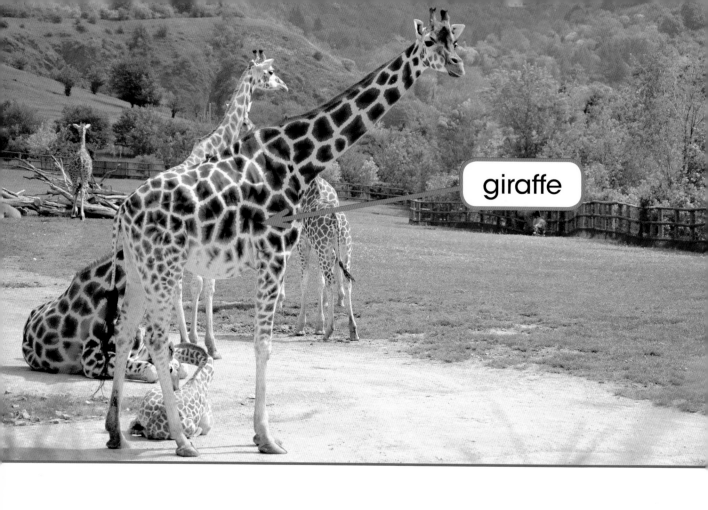

giraffe

Look at the giraffe.

Look at the snake.

parrot

Look at the parrot.

Look at the panda.

Look at the camel.

meerkat

Look at the meerkat.

Animal homes

Where do these animals live in the wild?

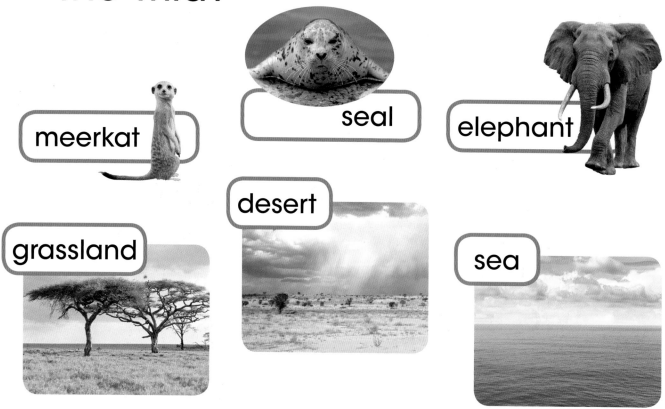

meerkat

seal

elephant

grassland

desert

sea

What am I?

I have claws.

I eat bamboo.

I have two arms and two legs.

I am covered in black and white fur.

Picture glossary

 crocodile

 koala

Index

22

Notes for teachers and parents

Before reading
Tuning in: Talk about animals the child has seen at a zoo or on TV.
  Which animal has a trunk? Which animal roars?

After reading
Recall and reflection: Which animals have stripes? Which animal has a hump?
Sentence knowledge: Help the child to count the number of words in each
  sentence.
Word knowledge (phonics): Encourage the child to point at the word 'at' on
  any page. Sound out the phonemes in the word 'a/t'. Ask the child to sound
  out each letter as they point at it and then blend the sounds together to
  make the word 'get'.
Word recognition: Challenge the child to race you to point at the word 'the' on
  any page.

Rounding off
Play a rhyming game: How many words can you think of that rhyme with 'zoo'
  (shoe, you, too, do, blue) etc.?

Word coverage

Sentence stem

Look at the _____.

High-frequency words

at
look
the

**Ask children to read
these words:**

lion	p7
seal	p9
hippo	p13
panda	p17

Topic words

camel
crocodile
elephant
giraffe
hippo
koala
lion
meerkat
monkey
panda
parrot
penguin
polar bear
seal
snake
tiger